You are something magical

Follow my story:

julian_blau FOLLOW

THE BAFFLED MAN

22430815R00072

Printed in Great Britain
by Amazon